21st Century
Basic Skills
Library

BABY ZOO ANIMALS
JAGUARS

by Katie Marsico

Cherry Lake Publishing • Ann Arbor, Michigan

3

Published in the United States of America
by Cherry Lake Publishing
Ann Arbor, Michigan
www.cherrylakepublishing.com

Content Adviser: Dr. Stephen S. Ditchkoff, Professor of Wildlife Sciences, Auburn University, Auburn, Alabama

Photo Credits: Cover and page 1, ©Arco Images GmbH/Alamy; page 4, ©Rechitan Sorin/Shutterstock, Inc.; pages 6 and 16, ©Zani Van Zyl/Dreamstime.com; page 8, ©Lajos Endrédi/Dreamstime.com; page 10, ©Elr.Sanchez/Shutterstock, Inc.; page 12, ©Graham Bloomfield/Shutterstock, Inc.; page 14, ©Paul Wood/Alamy; page 18, ©Joe Vogan/Alamy; page 20, ©Cynthia Kidwell/Shutterstock, Inc.

Library of Congress Cataloging-in-Publication Data
Marsico, Katie, 1980–
  Jaguars / by Katie Marsico.
    p. cm. — (21st century basic skills library) (Baby zoo animals)
  Includes bibliographical references and index.
  ISBN 978-1-61080-454-7 (lib. bdg.) — ISBN 978-1-61080-541-4 (e-book) — ISBN 978-1-61080-628-2 (pbk.)
  1. Jaguar—Infancy—Juvenile literature. 2. Zoo animals—Infancy—Juvenile literature. I. Title.
  SF408.6.J34M37 2013
  599.75'5—dc23   2012001943

Cherry Lake Publishing would like to acknowledge the work of The Partnership for 21st Century Skills. Please visit www.21stcenturyskills.org for more information.

Printed in the United States of America
Corporate Graphics Inc.
July 2012
CLFA11

TABLE OF CONTENTS

The Babies of Jaguars

Jaguars are among the largest cats in the world.

They are skilled hunters.

Jaguars will swim and climb to catch their **prey**.

Wild jaguars live in South America and Central America.

Others live in zoos around the world.

Jaguars usually have one to four **cubs** at a time.

Most jaguars are born with yellow fur and dark spots.

Some have black fur.

You can see their spots if you look closely.

A Jaguar's Day

Wild jaguars are usually more active when it is dark.

This is when they hunt. They eat anything from **tapirs** to fish.

Zookeepers feed jaguars meat.

Newborn cubs drink their mother's milk for about 5 months.

Jaguar cubs are quite playful.

They often wrestle and chase one another.

Zookeepers let the jaguars play with toys.

Mother jaguars teach their cubs important skills.

Their babies learn how to swim and climb trees.

Welcoming New Jaguar Cubs

Wild jaguars stay with their mothers for about 2 years.

They might be together for more or less time at zoos.

Young female jaguars become adults after 2 or 3 years. Then they are ready to have cubs of their own.

Then the zoo becomes home to new jaguar cubs!

Find Out More

BOOK
Gish, Melissa. *Jaguars*. Mankato, MN: Creative Education, 2012.

WEB SITE
San Diego Zoo—Jaguar
http://kids.sandiegozoo.org/animals/mammals/jaguar
Visit this site for a collection of photos and fast facts about jaguars.

Glossary

cubs (KUBZ) babies of certain animals, such as jaguars

jaguars (JAG-wahrz) large, spotted cats that live in South America and Central America

prey (PRAY) animals that are hunted and killed by other animals for food

tapirs (TAY-puhrz) large, piglike mammals that have hooves and a snout

zookeepers (ZOO-kee-purz) workers who take care of animals at zoos

Home and School Connection

Use this list of words from the book to help your child become a better reader. Word games and writing activities can help beginning readers reinforce literacy skills.

a	cats	home	months	see	trees
about	Central	how	more	skilled	usually
active	America	hunt	most	skills	welcoming
adults	chase	hunters	mother	some	when
after	climb	if	mother's	South	wild
among	closely	in	mothers	America	will
and	cubs	is	new	spots	with
another	dark	it	newborn	stay	world
anything	day	jaguar	not	swim	wrestle
are	drink	jaguar's	of	tapirs	years
around	eat	jaguars	often	teach	yellow
at	feed	largest	one	the	you
babies	female	learn	or	their	young
be	first	less	others	then	zoo
become	fish	let	own	they	zookeepers
becomes	for	live	play	this	zoos
black	four	look	playful	time	
born	from	meat	prey	to	
can	fur	might	quite	together	
catch	have	milk	ready	toys	

Fast Facts

Habitat: Swamps and forests, particularly rain forests
Range: Central and South America
Average Length: 5 to 6 feet (1.5 to 1.8 meters), with a tail between 27.5 and 36 inches (70 to 91 centimeters) long
Average Weight: 100 to 250 pounds (45 to 113 kilograms)
Life Span: 12 to 15 years

Index

About the Author

Katie Marsico is the author of more than 100 children's and young-adult reference books. She has seen jaguars at the zoo and thinks they are elegant, impressive cats.